People of the Bible

The Bible through stories and pictures

Moses
in the
Wilderness

Copyright © in this format Belitha Press Ltd, 1985

Text copyright © Catherine Storr 1985

Illustrations copyright © Jim Russell 1985

Art Director: Treld Bicknell

First published in the United States of America 1985
by Raintree Publishers Inc.
310 West Wisconsin Avenue, Milwaukee, Wisconsin 53203
in association with Belitha Press Ltd, London.

Conceived, designed and produced by Belitha Press Ltd,
2 Beresford Terrace, London N5 2DH

ISBN 0-8172-2039-9 (U.S.A.)

Library of Congress Cataloging in Publication Data

Storr, Catherine.
    Moses in the wilderness.

    (People of the Bible)
    Summary: Relates how Moses led the Children of
Israel out of Egypt and into the wilderness, where God
delivered the Ten Commandments to him.
        1. Moses (Biblical leader)—Juvenile literature.
2. Exodus, The—Juvenile literature.
3. Ten commandments—Juvenile literature.
4. Bible O.T.—Biography—Juvenile literature.
[1. Moses (Biblical leader) 2. Exodus, The.
3. Ten commandments.   4. Bible stories—O.T.]
I. Title.   II. Series.
BS580.M6S757   1985   222'.1209505   85-12285

ISBN 0-8172-2039-9

First published in Great Britain in hardback 1985
by Franklin Watts Ltd,
12a Golden Square, London W1R 4BA

3 4 5 6 7 8 9 10 11 12 13   98 97 96 95 94 93 92 91 90 89 88

Moses
in the
Wilderness

Retold by Catherine Storr
Pictures by Jim Russell

Raintree Childrens Books
Milwaukee
Belitha Press Limited • London

After the last of the plagues which God had sent to the Egyptians, Pharaoh told the Children of Israel to leave Egypt as soon as they could. They took jewels of gold and silver from the Egyptians.

"Go quickly," the Egyptians said, "or we shall all be dead men."

The Israelites left at once. They took their bread dough with them without waiting for it to rise, so it was unleavened bread. By day they followed a pillar of cloud, and by night a pillar of fire.

After they had left, Pharaoh's heart was hardened again. He sent an army to bring them back to Egypt.

When the Children of Israel saw Pharaoh's chariots pursuing them, they cried, "Were there no graves for us in Egypt? You have led us out to die in the wilderness."

But Moses said, "Fear not. Keep still and God will save you."

Moses stretched out his hand over the sea, and God sent a strong east wind to blow all night. In the morning, the sea parted and there was dry land between two walls of water. The Children of Israel went safely through.

But when the Egyptians followed, Moses stretched out his hand again and the waters returned and rushed over the Egyptians. Every man was drowned.

As they went on through the desert the people became hungry. They complained to Moses, "In Egypt we had plenty to eat. Here we shall die of starvation."

Moses said, "God has heard you complain. He will give you meat to eat in the evening, and bread in the morning."

That evening the ground was covered with quails. The next morning there was manna scattered all over the camp.

As the Israelites journeyed in the wilderness, they found no water. They were very thirsty, and they complained again to Moses.

God told Moses, "Go and stand before the rock of Horeb and strike it with your rod. Then water will flow and my people shall drink."

13

But now the Amalekites came to fight the Israelites. Moses called Joshua, the son of Nun, to lead the army.

"I will stand on that hill, with the rod of God in my hand," Moses said.

Sometimes one side won and sometimes the other. Moses found that if he lifted up his hands, the Israelites were victorious. If his hands fell down, the Amalekites won. He sat on a stone, and Aaron and Hur held up his hands for him until Joshua had won the battle.

15

After three months in the wilderness the Children of Israel came to the desert of Sinai. God called Moses up into the mountain. He said, "If my people obey my commandments, they shall be a holy nation and my chosen people. Go down and tell them to be ready for me on the third day."

On the third day there was thunder and lightning, and a black cloud hung over the mountain. The voice of the trumpet sounded. The people trembled and the mountain quaked. God said to Moses, "Come up the mountain again, and I will give you my laws."

God gave these commandments for his people: You shall have no other gods, but Me. You shall not make idols. You shall worship the Lord, the one God. You shall not swear, nor steal, nor kill each other. You must honor your fathers and mothers. You shall not work on the Sabbath, the seventh day. You shall not say wrong things about your neighbor, nor try to steal his wife. You shall not envy anything that belongs to a neighbor—his land, or his cattle.

God wrote these laws on two tablets of stone.

Moses stayed on the mountain for forty days and forty nights. While he was gone, the people came to Aaron and said, "We don't know where Moses is, or if he will ever come back. Make us a god to lead us."

So Aaron made a statue of a calf, all of gold. He said, "Here is your god. Worship him."

On the mountain, God said to Moses, "Go down to the people. They are worshipping an idol instead of me. I shall punish them."

Moses said, "Lord God, do not be angry with your people. Remember Abraham and Isaac and Jacob and your promises to them."

As Moses went down the mountain, he heard the shouts of the people below. When he saw the Children of Israel dancing round the golden calf and worshipping it, he was very angry.

He threw the two stone tablets to the ground and they broke into pieces.

Moses said to Aaron, "What have the people done to you that you should make them sin in this way?"

Aaron said, "Don't be so angry. The people meant no harm. We did not know where you were, so they asked me to make them a new god."

Moses stood at the gate of the camp and said, "Whoever is on God's side, let him come to me here." All the sons of the tribe of Levi came to Moses' side.

Moses told them to kill everyone who would not obey God. Many people died. Then Moses pleaded with God to forgive the Children of Israel their sin in making the golden calf.

God said to Moses, "Now, go on into the wilderness. I will send an angel before you and I will bring my people into a land flowing with milk and honey."

The people watching saw the pillar of cloud and knew that God was speaking to Moses as a friend.

Moses asked God, "May I see your face in glory?"

God said, "No. That would be too much for you. Stand on a rock, and I will pass by, and you will see a part of my glory."

God told Moses to make two new tablets of stone. He said, "I will write my commandments on them."

Early the next morning, Moses went up to the top of Mount Sinai. God told him to lead the Children of Israel to live in Canaan.

When Moses came down from Mount Sinai where he had been talking with God, the skin of his face shone, so that the people were afraid to come near him.

Now the fine craftsmen of the people began to make the Tabernacle ready for the Ark. The Tabernacle tent had curtains of blue and purple and scarlet linen, embroidered with golden cherubs.

Inside the Tabernacle tent was a box made of acacia wood, to hold the tablets of stone. This was the Ark.

Aaron and his sons were the priests of the Tabernacle. They made a burnt offering on the golden altar and the glory of the Lord was over the Tabernacle.

The Desert Wanderings

Mt. Ararat

Tarshish

R. Tigris

Nineveh

R. Euphrates

Mediterranean Sea

Nazareth

Sea of Galilee

Joppa

Jerusalem

Bethlehem

Hebron

Canaan

Land of Goshen

WILDERNESS

Succoth

Bitter Lakes

Memphis

S I N A I

The exact place where the
Children of Israel crossed
the water and escaped from
the Egyptians is not known.
They might have crossed a
lake, or a narrow inlet of
the sea. Some scholars
think it might have been
called 'the Reed Sea' and
that over the years this was
muddled with 'the Red Sea'.

E G Y P T

Mt Sinai/Horeb

Thebes